Cha

by Iain Gray

Lang**Syne**
PUBLISHING
WRITING *to* REMEMBER

LangSyne

PUBLISHING

WRITING *to* REMEMBER

79 Main Street, Newtongrange,
Midlothian EH22 4NA
Tel: 0131 344 0414   Fax: 0845 075 6085
E-mail: info@lang-syne.co.uk
www.langsyneshop.co.uk

Design by Dorothy Meikle
Printed by Ricoh Print Scotland
© Lang Syne Publishers Ltd 2013

ISBN 978-1-85217-486-6

Chambers

MOTTO:
I hope.

CREST:
Three green holly leaves atop a ducal coronet
(and)
A demi-eagle atop a ducal coronet
(and)
A bear, muzzled.

NAME variations include:
Chalmairs
Challmers
Chalmers
Chamers

Chapter one:

The origins of popular surnames

by George Forbes and Iain Gray

If you don't know where you came from, you won't know where you're going **is a frequently quoted observation and one that has a particular resonance today when there has been a marked upsurge in interest in genealogy, with increasing numbers of people curious to trace their family roots.**

Main sources for genealogical research include census returns and official records of births, marriages and deaths – and the key to unlocking the detail they contain is obviously a family surname, one that has been 'inherited' and passed from generation to generation.

No matter our station in life, we all have a surname – but it was not until about the middle of the fourteenth century that the practice of being identified by a particular surname became commonly established throughout the British Isles.

Previous to this, it was normal for a person to be identified through the use of only a forename.

But as population gradually increased and there were many more people with the same forename, surnames were adopted to distinguish one person, or community, from another.

Many common English surnames are patronymic in origin, meaning they stem from the forename of one's father – with 'Johnson,' for example, indicating 'son of John.'

It was the Normans, in the wake of their eleventh century conquest of Anglo-Saxon England, a pivotal moment in the nation's history, who first brought surnames into usage – although it was a gradual process.

For the Normans, these were names initially based on the title of their estates, local villages and chateaux in France to distinguish and identify these landholdings.

Such grand descriptions also helped enhance the prestige of these warlords and generally glorify their lofty positions high above the humble serfs slaving away below in the pecking order who had only single names, often with Biblical connotations as in Pierre and Jacques.

The only descriptive distinctions among the peasantry concerned their occupations, like 'Pierre the swineherd' or 'Jacques the ferryman.'

Roots of surnames that came into usage in England not only included Norman-French, but also Old French, Old Norse, Old English, Middle English, German, Latin, Greek, Hebrew and the Gaelic languages of the Celts.

The Normans themselves were originally Vikings, or 'Northmen', who raided, colonised and eventually settled down around the French coastline.

The had sailed up the Seine in their longboats in 900AD under their ferocious leader Rollo and ruled the roost in north eastern France before sailing over to conquer England in 1066 under Duke William of Normandy – better known to posterity as William the Conqueror, or King William I of England.

Granted lands in the newly-conquered England, some of their descendants later acquired territories in Wales, Scotland and Ireland – taking not only their own surnames, but also the practice of adopting a surname, with them.

But it was in England where Norman rule and custom first impacted, particularly in relation to the adoption of surnames.

This is reflected in the famous *Domesday Book*, a massive survey of much of England and Wales, ordered by William I, to determine who owned what, what it was worth and therefore how much they were liable to pay in taxes to the voracious Royal Exchequer.

Completed in 1086 and now held in the National Archives in Kew, London, 'Domesday' was an Old English word meaning 'Day of Judgement.'

This was because, in the words of one contemporary chronicler, "its decisions, like those of the Last Judgement, are unalterable."

It had been a requirement of all those English landholders – from the richest to the poorest – that they identify themselves for the purposes of the survey and for future reference by means of a surname.

This is why the *Domesday Book*, although written in Latin as was the practice for several centuries with both civic and ecclesiastical records, is an invaluable source for the early appearance of a wide range of English surnames.

Several of these names were coined in connection with occupations.

These include Baker and Smith, while Cooks, Chamberlains, Constables and Porters were to be found carrying out duties in large medieval households.

The church's influence can be found in names such as Bishop, Friar and Monk while the popular name of Bennett derives from the late fifth to mid-sixth century Saint Benedict, founder of the Benedictine order of monks.

The early medical profession is represented by Barber, while businessmen produced names that include Merchant and Sellers.

Down at the village watermill, the names that cropped up included Millar/Miller, Walker and Fuller, while other self-explanatory trades included Cooper, Tailor, Mason and Wright.

Even the scenery was utilised as in Moor, Hill, Wood and Forrest – while the hunt and the chase supplied names that include Hunter, Falconer, Fowler and Fox.

Colours are also a source of popular surnames, as in Black, Brown, Gray/Grey, Green and White, and would have denoted the colour of the clothing the person habitually wore or, apart from the obvious exception of 'Green', one's hair colouring or even complexion.

The surname Red developed into Reid, while

Blue was rare and no-one wanted to be associated with yellow.

Rather self-important individuals took surnames that include Goodman and Wiseman, while physical attributes crept into surnames such as Small and Little.

Many families proudly boast the heraldic device known as a Coat of Arms, as featured on our front cover.

The central motif of the Coat of Arms would originally have been what was borne on the shield of a warrior to distinguish himself from others on the battlefield.

Not featured on the Coat of Arms, but highlighted on page three, is the family motto and related crest – with the latter frequently different from the central motif.

Adding further variety to the rich cultural heritage that is represented by surnames is the appearance in recent times in lists of the 100 most common names found in England of ones that include Khan, Patel and Singh – names that have proud roots in the vast sub-continent of India.

Echoes of a far distant past can still be found in our surnames and they can be borne with pride in commemoration of our forebears.

Chapter two:

Power and conquest

A name derived from the Old French 'de la chambre', meaning 'of the chamber', 'Chambers' has been present throughout the British Isles since at least the eleventh century.

An occupational surname, it indicated someone who worked in the household 'chambers', or rooms of a monarch or wealthy nobleman – in the role of someone entrusted with either the royal treasury or a nobleman's household finances.

Although some sources assert the name was present in Britain for some period before the eleventh century, the available evidence shows it became particularly common in the aftermath of the Norman Conquest of 1066.

By 1066, Anglo-Saxon England had become a nation with several powerful competitors to the throne.

In what were extremely complex family, political and military machinations, the monarch was Harold II, who had succeeded to the throne following the death of Edward the Confessor.

But his right to the throne was contested by two powerful competitors – his brother-in-law King Harold Hardrada of Norway, in alliance with Tostig, Harold II's brother, and Duke William II of Normandy.

In what has become known as The Year of Three Battles, Hardrada invaded England and gained victory over the English king on September 20th at the battle of Fulford, in Yorkshire.

Five days later, however, Harold II decisively defeated his brother-in-law and brother at the battle of Stamford Bridge.

But Harold had little time to celebrate his victory, having to immediately march south from Yorkshire to encounter a mighty invasion force, led by Duke William of Normandy, which had landed at Hastings, in East Sussex.

Harold's battle-hardened but exhausted force of Anglo-Saxon soldiers confronted the Normans on October 25th in a battle subsequently depicted on the Bayeux tapestry – a 23ft. long strip of embroidered linen thought to have been commissioned eleven years after the event by the Norman Odo of Bayeux.

It was at the top of Senlac Hill that Harold drew up a strong defensive position, building a shield wall to repel Duke William's cavalry and infantry.

The Normans suffered heavy losses, but through a combination of the deadly skill of their archers and the ferocious determination of their cavalry they eventually won the day.

Anglo-Saxon morale had collapsed on the battlefield as word spread through the ranks that Harold had been killed – the Bayeux Tapestry depicting this as having happened when the English king was struck by an arrow to the head.

Amidst the carnage of the battlefield, it was difficult to identify Harold – the last of the Anglo-Saxon kings.

Some sources assert William ordered his body to be thrown into the sea, while others state it was secretly buried at Waltham Abbey.

What is known with certainty, however, is that William in celebration of his great victory founded Battle Abbey, near the site of the battle, ordering that the altar be sited on the spot where Harold was believed to have fallen.

William was declared King of England on December 25th, and what followed was the complete subjugation of his Anglo-Saxon subjects.

Those Normans such as the Chambers who had fought on his behalf were rewarded with the lands of Anglo-Saxons, many of whom sought exile abroad as mercenaries.

Within an astonishingly short space of time, Norman manners, customs and law were imposed on England – laying the basis for what subsequently became established 'English' custom and practice.

It was following the Conquest that a John de Chambre is recorded as having been rewarded for his support with the grant of lands at Llewenne, in the modern day Welsh area of Denbighshire.

In common with other Norman families rewarded with the grant of lands in Wales, the Chambers became known as Cambro-Normans.

'Cambro' comes from the Welsh, and 'Cambro-Norman' describes those Welsh knights of Norman origin, such as bearers of what became the Chambers name, who invaded Ireland in 1171.

This was when England's Henry II agreed to aid Dermot MacMurrough, king of the Irish province of Leinster, in his bloody bid to usurp the power of Rory O'Connor, king of the province of Connacht.

Although agreeing to help MacMurrough, Henry distanced himself from direct involvement by delegating his Norman subjects in Wales with the task.

With an eye on rich booty, plunder and lands,

Cambro-Normans such as the ancestors of some bearers of the Chambers name today, were only too eager to obey their sovereign's wishes and lend MacMurrough their formidable military skills.

The mighty Norman war machine soon moved into action, and so disciplined and ferocious was their onslaught on the forces of Rory O'Connor and his allies that they soon captured Dublin and other strategically important territories.

It was now that a nervous Henry II began to take cold feet over the venture, realising that he may have had inadvertently created a powerful rival in the form of a separate Norman kingdom in Ireland.

Accordingly, he landed on the island, at Waterford, in October of 1171 with the aim of curbing the power of his Cambro-Norman barons such as bearers of the Chambers name.

But protracted warfare between the king and his barons was averted when the barons submitted to the royal will – giving homage and promising allegiance in return for holding the territories they had conquered in the king's name.

This is why the Chambers name came to be found in not only England and Wales but also, after 1171, in Ireland.

Bearers of the Chambers name came to figure prominently in the historical record.

A friend of the English poet, essayist, biographer and lexicographer Dr Samuel Johnson, Sir Robert Chambers was the lawyer, academic and colonial administrator born in Newcastle upon Tyne in 1737.

The son of a lawyer, he was called to the bar himself at the age of 24 while in 1766 he was appointed to the prestigious post of Vinerian Professor of Law at the University of Oxford – helped in good part by his friend Dr Johnson who had provided glowing references recommending him for the post.

Later serving as Chief Justice of Bengal, the East Indian climate eventually took its toll on his health and he retired to the more congenial climate of the south of France.

Married to Frances Witton, a daughter of the English sculptor Joseph Witton, he died in 1803.

One of his seven children married John Macdonald, the youngest son of Flora Macdonald who is immortalised for having helped Charles Edward Stuart, better known to posterity as Bonnie Prince Charlie, to evade capture in the aftermath of the abortive Jacobite Rising of 1745.

One bearer of the Chambers name who had a particularly inquiring mind was the English writer and encyclopaedist Ephraim Chambers, born in 1680 in Kendal, Westmoreland.

Apprenticed for a time to a globe-maker in London, he later developed an ambitious plan for what became his *Universal Dictionary of Arts and Sciences*, also known as the *Cyclopaedia*.

It was while also working for the Literary magazine and with John Martyn on a translation of the *History and Memoirs of the Royal Academy of Sciences of Paris* that he completed his prized project of the universal dictionary.

Published in two volumes twelve years before his death in 1740, it was dedicated to George II.

He was interred in the cloisters of Westminster Abbey in recognition of his great achievement.

Chapter three:

Thirst for knowledge

Not only of inquiring literary and scientific minds but also pioneers in the world of publishing, two nineteenth century bearers of the Chambers name left a legacy that survives to this day.

They were the brothers William and Robert Chambers, born respectively in 1800 and 1802 in the town of Peebles in the Scottish Borders.

Even from birth they were marked out as being 'different' – both being born with six fingers on each hand and six toes on each foot.

This abnormality was successfully corrected through surgical operations on the older brother, but Robert was left partially lame.

Their father James was a cotton manufacturer, but became a draper after he was forced to abandon his business with the introduction of the power loom.

Declared bankrupt in 1813 after he was unable to recoup credit he had given to French prisoners-of-war who had been paroled and stationed in Peebles, he moved the family to Edinburgh.

It was here that William became a bookseller's apprentice, while Robert continued his formal education until the age of 16.

William was able to establish his own printing and publishing enterprise in 1819, while Robert had become a bookstall-keeper on Leith Walk – with his first stock being some old books belonging to his father.

Both businesses prospered and the brothers decided to enter into partnership – with the launch in 1821 of the fortnightly magazine *Edinburgh Literary Amusement*.

Its success allowed the brothers to rapidly expand their printing and publishing business.

In 1822 they published the best-selling *Illustrations of the Author of Waverley*, followed two years later by *Traditions of Edinburgh* and in 1825 with *Walks in Edinburgh*.

With a keen interest in history, science and antiquities, Robert was the author of these works along with others that include the four-volume *Biographical Dictionary of Eminent Scotsmen*, the four-volume *The Life and Works of Robert Burns* and, published between 1859 and 1861, *The Domestic Annals of Scotland*.

Launching the weekly publication *Chambers*

Edinburgh Journal and trading as the book publishing company of *W. and R. Chambers Publishers*, the brothers were also responsible for *Chamber's Encyclopaedia* and a number of other publications that include *The Chambers Dictionary*.

Robert's noted and still best-selling *The Book of Days*, a miscellany of antiquities in connection with the calendar, was published in two volumes between 1862 and 1864.

William Chambers, known by the time of his death in 1883 as William Chambers of Glenormiston, also served from 1865 to 1869 as Lord Provost of Edinburgh and was instrumental in a number of major civic works that included the restoration of St Giles Cathedral.

The city's Chambers Street, graced by a statue of him, is named in his honour.

William Chambers appears to have had the main 'business brains' that made *W. and R. Chambers* so successful, while his brother Robert's contribution came in the form of his thirst for knowledge, exhaustive research and prolific authorship.

It is thought that his work on *The Book of Days* exacerbated his fragile health and contributed to his death in 1871.

He recalled towards the end of his life how as a young boy he had found a complete set of an edition of *Encyclopaedia Britannica* in a chest in his father's attic.

He read and re-read the collection over a period of many years and said how he remembered feeling "a profound thankfulness that such a convenient collection of human knowledge existed, and here it was spread out like a well-plenished table before me."

His thirst for knowledge extended to the field of geology and in 1844 he was elected a fellow of the Geological Society of London – having four years earlier being elected as a member of the Royal Society of Edinburgh.

His geological work, *Ancient Sea Margins*, was published in 1848, while his *Vestiges of the Natural History of Creation* had been published anonymously in 1844, through a Manchester-based publisher, and his authorship not acknowledged until some years after his death.

This was because, proposing the highly controversial theory at the time that 'God' may not have been responsible for creation, it may have damaged the highly respected and successful *W. and R. Chambers* 'brand name.'

The family business was later carried on by his son, Robert Chambers, born in 1832 and who died in 1888.

It was under his direction that the business continued to prosper and expand.

Taking over the publishing company of *Harrap* in the early 1990s, the business originally founded by William and Robert Chambers continues to flourish as *Chambers Harrap Publishing* – publishing a range of subjects that include dictionaries, thesauruses and language reference.

From the world of publishing to the Church, Oswald J. Chambers was the Baptist minister who died during the First World War after selflessly refusing to take up a hospital bed needed by wounded soldiers.

Although suffering from the agony of a ruptured appendix, he underwent the pain for three days before seeking medical attention.

This was in November of 1917 in the aftermath of the disastrous Gallipoli Campaign when hundreds of badly wounded Australian and New Zealand (ANZAC) troops were evacuated for treatment in Zeitoun, Egypt.

Eventually staggering into hospital, he

refused to take up a hospital bed and died shortly afterwards.

Born in Aberdeen in 1874, it was in 1915 that he had been accepted as a military chaplain and assigned to Egypt.

Married to Gertrude Hobbs, better known as "Biddy", he was the author of more than thirty religious devotional books that include his best-known *My Utmost for the Highest*.

From the Church to the civil service and industry, Sir Paul Chambers was responsible for devising the Pay As You Earn (PAYE) taxation system used in the United Kingdom to this day.

Born in London in 1904 and a graduate of the London School of Economics (LSE), he entered the Inland Revenue Service and six years before the outbreak of the Second World War in 1939 was appointed Income Tax Advisor in the Government of India.

Later serving throughout the war as Director of Statistics and Intelligence in the Inland Revenue, it was during this period that he devised the PAYE system.

Appointed financial director of Imperial Chemical Industries (ICI) in 1948, he served as the company's chairman from 1960 to 1968 before taking up the post of chairman of Royal Insurance.

Also president of the Royal Statistical Society from 1964 to 1965, and who's Chambers Medal is named in his honour, he died in 1981.

In the world of politics, George Chambers served as the second Prime Minister of Trinidad and Tobago between 1981 and 1986.

Born in Port of Spain in 1928 and a member of the People's National Movement (PNM), he died in 1997.

One bearer of the proud name of Chambers whose legacy survives to this day in the form of a number of landmarks that grace the skylines of New York and other American cities was the architect Walter Chambers.

Born in 1866 in Brooklyn, New York, the son of a prominent attorney, he graduated from Yale University at the age of 21 and went on to study architecture at the Ecole des Beaux Arts in Paris.

One of his fellow students in Paris was Ernest Flagg, with whom he formed an architectural partnership in 1894.

They were responsible through their partnership for New York's Singer Building, which between 1908 and 1909 held the record as the world's tallest building.

Other major works include the Corcoran Gallery of Art in Washington, D.C. and the Washington State Capitol.

A member of the American Institute of Architects, he died in 1945, after having established a school of architecture in New York that produced other famed architects who include Leonard B. Schultze, architect of the city's famed Waldorf Astoria Hotel.

He was a brother of Robert Chambers, a noted American author in the genre of supernatural fiction.

Born in 1865 in Brooklyn, New York, his many works include the 1894 *In the Quarter* and the 1904 *In Search of the Unknown* – while his 1895 *The King in Yellow* is recognised as one of the most important woks of the genre; he died in 1933.

Chapter four:

On the world stage

In the world of popular music, Guy Chambers is the English songwriter, musician and record producer best known for his work with the singer, songwriter and entertainer Robbie Williams.

Born in London in 1963, he studied musical composition and piano at the Guildhall School of Music.

Meeting with Robbie Williams in 1997, he collaborated with him on a string of international hit albums and singles that include *Angels*, *Let Me Entertain You*, *Rock DJ* and *Millennium*.

He is the recipient of a number of awards that include three Ivor Novello Awards and three BRITS.

Born in 1976, **Kasey Chambers** is the Australian country music singer and songwriter whose cover of the Cyndi Lauper song *True Colors* became the theme song of the 2003 Rugby World Cup.

From a musical background that includes her father, the steel guitar player Bill Chambers and her brother the musician and record producer Nash

Chambers, she has also enjoyed chart success with singles that include the 2008 *Monkey on a Wire* and her 2011 *Beautiful Mess*.

Born in 1967, **Sandra Chambers**, also known by her recording name of Sandy, is the British dance music vocalist of the electronic dance genre known as Eurodance.

Her best-selling tracks include the 2002 *Miss You* and the 2009 *Brighter*.

In the much different musical genre of jazz, **Paul Chambers** was the double bassist recognised as having developed the importance of the instrument throughout the 1950s and up until his death in 1969.

Born in 1935 in Pittsburgh, Pennsylvania, he recorded with other jazz luminaries who include John Coltrane, Art Pepper, Thelonius Monk and Miles Davis.

Taking up the drumsticks at the age of four and playing in Baltimore clubs only two years later, **Dennis Chambers** is the renowned American drummer, born in 1959, who has performed and recorded with artists and bands who include John Scofield, Santana, John McLaughlin and Parliament/Funkadelic.

Born in 1854 in Newport, Pennsylvania, **William Paris Chambers** was the American cornet soloist, composer and bandleader whose best known works include the marches *The Boys of the Old Brigade* and *Chicago Tribune*; he died in 1913.

From music to acting, Faune Alecia Chambers is the American actress better known as **Faune A. Chambers**.

Born in Florida in 1976, her film credits include the 2002 comedy *Goldmember*, the 2004 *White Chicks* and, from 2007, *Epic Movie*.

Born in 1964 in Doncaster, Yorkshire, **Emma Chambers** is the actress whose British television credits include the role of Alice Tinker in the sitcom *The Vicar of Dibley*, while she also starred as Honey Thacker in the 1999 film *Notting Hill*.

Best known for his roles of Wilder in the television series *The Latest Buzz* and as Eli Goldsworthy in *Degrassi*, **Munro Chambers** is the Canadian actor born in 1990.

His film credits include the 2004 *Godsend*.

A former fashion model for Calvin Klein, **Justin W. Chambers** is the American actor best known for his role from 2005 of Dr Alex Karev in the television medical drama *Grey's Anatomy*.

Born in 1970 in Springfield, Ohio, his other television credits include *Cold Case*.

On British television screens, **Tom Chambers** is the actor best known for his role of Sam Strachan in the popular medical drama *Holby City*.

Born in 1977 in Darley Dale, Derbyshire, in 2008 he won the sixth season of BBC's *Strictly Come Dancing* with his professional dance partner Camilla Dallerup.

From the world of acting to the written word, **Aidan Chambers** is the former teacher and monk whose best-selling books for children and young adults include his 1967 *Cycle Smash* and the *Dance Sequence* series.

Born in 1934 in Co. Durham and President of the School Library Association from 2003 to 2006, he is the recipient of a 2000 Hans Christian Andersen Award 'in recognition of the distinguished body of his writing.'

From the written word to the sciences, **Robert Chambers** was the American biologist who invented instruments to dissect living cells.

Born in 1881 and a president of the Union of American Biological Sciences and the American Society of Zoologists, he died in 1957.

Bearers of the Chambers name have also excelled, and continue to excel, in the highly competitive world of sport.

Born in 1975 and an inductee of the Canadian Sports Hall of Fame, **Carlton Chambers** is the retired sprint athlete who was a member of the Canadian team that won the gold medal in the 4 x 400-metres relay at the 1996 Olympics in Atlanta.

Setting a Junior World record in 1997 of 10.06 seconds in the 100-metres sprint, **Dwain Chambers** is the British track sprinter born in London in 1978.

The winner of championship medals at both European and World level and recognised as one of the fastest sprinters in the history of athletics, he is nevertheless no stranger to controversy.

He received a two-year athletics ban and a lifetime Olympic ban in 2003 after testing positive for a banned performance enhancing drug.

The Olympic ban was overturned in 2012, allowing him to compete in the Olympic Games in London of that year – but he failed to qualify for the final of the 100-metres sprint.

From the athletics track to the fields of European football, **Luke Chambers** is the English centre-back, born in 1985 in Kettering, Northants, who has played for teams that include Northampton Town, Nottingham Forest and, from 2012, Ipswich Town.

Born in 1990 in Leicester, **Ashley Chambers** is the winger and striker who, in addition to playing for teams that include Leicester City and York City, also played for the England Under-16, Under-17, Under-18 and Under-19 teams.

In American football, **Chris Chambers** is the retired wide receiver of the National Football League (NFL).

Born in 1978 in Cleveland, Ohio, he played for teams that include the Miami Dolphins, San Diego Chargers and, from 2009 to 2010, the Kansas City Chiefs.

Developing his arm and chest muscles through the physically demanding task of stirring molten iron with a ladle while working in an ironworks, **Robert Chambers** became a famed English rower.

Born in 1832 in St Anthony's, near Newcastle, he was the world champion in the discipline of sculling from 1859 to 1865 and from 1866 until his death in 1868.

His death, at the age of 36, was from tuberculosis – thought to have been brought on from his lungs having been damaged in the grime and heat of the ironworks where he had earlier worked.

An inductee of the International Tennis Hall of Fame, **Dorothea Lambert Chambers**, born Dorothea Douglass in 1878 in Ealing, West London, was a prominent figure in the early days of ladies tennis.

Making her Wimbledon debut at the age of 22, she later went on to win an impressive seven ladies singles titles between 1903 and 1914.

Known professionally as Dorothea Lambert Chambers after her marriage, she was also the author of *Tennis for Ladies*, published in 1910.

Containing photographic illustrations of tennis techniques, it also offers advice for lady players on proper equipment and attire.

This was at a time when female players were required to take to the tennis court demurely and uncomfortably dressed in long-sleeved blouses, buttoned to the neck, and voluminous skirts down to the ankles.

Also a winner of the gold medal for the ladies singles at the 1908 Olympics, she died in 1960.